MW01122125

By **Taryn Rose**

BUS STOPS & BICYCLES

A handbook for Single Ladies

RUBY'S HOUSE
PUBLISHING

Scriptures taken from the Holy Bible, New International Version®, NIV®. Copyright © 1973, 1978, 1984 by Biblica, Inc.™ Used by permission of Zondervan. All rights reserved worldwide. www.zondervan.com

Published in Melbourne, Australia by Ruby's House Publishing

Edited by Mari Atkinson
Cover Art and Illustrations by Taryn Rose

ISBN 978-0-646-54412-0

RUBY'S HOUSE
PUBLISHING

Dedication:

This book is dedicated to all of my housemates, past and present (I'm counting you too Ruth, for all of those nights you slept on the couch!) You are all truly amazing women and I'm so thankful to you for allowing me to talk out this book before I ever started writing it.

I am a woman who follows Jesus and I am not married I am old enough to have been to over 30 weddings and young enough to still be invited to the occasional 21st I have met The One more than once and I have realized, more than once, that I was mistaken I have cried myself to sleep I have felt deep loneliness I have rolled my eyes at insensitive comments by well-meaning people I have known jealousy I have wondered if there was something wrong with me I have been frustrated by clichéd answers to big questions I have read all of the books I have seen people get married I have seen marriages fall apart I haven't given up on marriage In fact, I believe in it fiercely I am not a feminist or one of those independent types But I refuse to wait around hoping to one day be rescued I refuse to believe that I am 'less than' (less attractive, less fun, less useful to God) because I am not married Don't get me wrong... I am not bitter or angry Far from it I have just found a different path I haven't got all the answers And it still hurts sometimes But I have learned a few things along the way So I wrote them down Because I thought that you might find them helpful too I hope you do

Taryn xo

A few things that you need to know *before* we begin

This book *isn't...* a 3-step plan for finding a man. Sorry. None of my plans have been all that successful (to be honest, they haven't worked *at all*), so I'm not really qualified to write about them. If I do have any success I'll write a sequel...

This book *isn't...* going to tell you that you're a beautiful princess and you should wait in your white tower until Prince Charming comes on his horse to whisk you away into Ever After.

This book *isn't...* based on highly accurate statistics and research. I've never been much of a details girl. I prefer to go with the *vibe of the thing*.

This book *isn't...* very long. I don't usually make it to the end of non-fiction books (I have a theory that the important stuff is in the first two chapters and then it's just padding to make the book look more credible). So, I've tried to keep this as short and sweet as possible and I've drawn pictures to make it more interesting. I always find pictures help.

This book *isn't...* for everyone. Some of you will get it and some of you will probably think I'm weird. That's ok. If you don't get what I'm talking about maybe just enjoy the pictures and pass the book on to a friend.

This book *isn't...* going to tell you how to *prepare yourself* for your husband. It's about how to *live your life* right now.

This book *isn't...* the all-inclusive answer to everything you may face as a single girl. It wasn't written to answer all of your questions, but to get you to start asking your own. It's time that we started talking about this stuff and I thought that if there was a book about it, maybe we wouldn't feel as embarrassed or ashamed admitting that sometimes singleness is hard and there isn't always a clear path mapped out on how to do it well.

Introduction

Sometimes, I catch the bus to work. I'm a bit of a people-watcher and over time I've found it really interesting to observe bus stop culture. Everyone seems to have their own bus waiting routine. Some people stand close to the curb, anxiously peering into the distance, hoping to be the first to catch a glimpse of the bus. Others pass the time by playing with their phone, acting disinterested, glancing up only occasionally to see if the bus is in sight. Then there are the ones who are running late - they check their watches constantly and usually pace back and forth from the curb to the seat, never standing still. And then there are the ones who always manage to arrive at the very last moment, hair all out of place and completely out of breath, inwardly vowing to get there earlier next time.

Over time I have realized that there is one thing that unites all of the people who wait at the bus stop: no matter what they are doing, they are all *waiting*. Each one of them waits for the bus to come and take them in the direction they are heading.

Another thing I've noticed is that no one seems to enjoy waiting for the bus - probably because one never knows quite when the bus will arrive, how full it will be or if it will arrive at all! Admittedly, there are some distractions that can make the wait easier: talking to the other people at the stop, reading a book, or listening to music. Essentially though, everyone is stranded at the bus stop and completely dependent on the bus to show up to move them along to their destination.

For years, I lived my life at a bus stop.

For years, I lived my life at a bus stop. The 'Husband' bus stop. I stood. I waited. I looked anxiously towards the road, expecting, hoping, willing my bus to come along. How else was I to get to my destination except by the bus? (Translation: how was I meant to live the life God had called me to live and reach my destiny without a husband?) I waited and waited and waited. My eyes followed every passing vehicle, with one question always hanging in the air: Was this one The One I had been waiting for? After a while I began to have other questions too. Was there a delay with the traffic? Had there been some kind of accident that was holding everything up? Or worse still, had the bus passed me by without my even noticing it?

I was so focussed on waiting for a man that I put many things in my life on hold. I spent all of my time looking out at the road and forgot to even consider my destination. The only question that was important to me was, 'When is my man coming?'

Sometimes I ride my bike to work. I love riding my pushy. It's an old bike that probably deserved the scrapheap before I convinced my Dad to help me restore it one summer. If you picture the kind of bike that you got around on when you were a kid, it looks pretty much like that – complete with cane basket, pink handle bar grips and a bell. I even wanted to put some spoky-dokies on the wheels in order to hear that clickity-clack as I rode along, but the general consensus amongst my friends was that that would have been taking things too far. It may be that I still ride on the sidewalk and the bike I ride is fairly childish, but when I ride, I still get the same rush I did as a kid. When I am riding down a hill, and the wind is sweeping past me, I still have that delicious moment where I close my eyes for a second and imagine that I am flying.

Cycling offers such a sense of freedom and independence, mainly because I ride at whatever pace I feel like. (Monday mornings are generally a little on the sluggish side, whereas Friday afternoons see me set a cracking pace.) What's more, I can change the route at any time. I enjoy the feeling of pushing the pedals up and down and propelling myself forwards, knowing that I am not dependent on anyone else to get me where I am going.

I must admit that quite often I find riding my bike a more difficult prospect than waiting for the bus. Riding equals puffing and sweating, burning muscles and changes of clothes. But there are also benefits in riding that catching the bus just doesn't provide – overall fitness, toned muscles and a sense of satisfaction and achievement in knowing that I have actively moved myself towards my destination.

In my life, I have made a decision to *ride*, to keep moving forward towards my destination. I'm done waiting for the 'Husband' bus. I still want to get married, but I'm not going to *wait around* for a husband to come along before I begin living my life or pursuing my God-given destiny.

It's relatively easy to *wait around* for a man. If we choose to wait, there's less need to make major life decisions. We can instead store them away in the 'Later' cupboard until there is someone to make them with.

> *Choosing to ride does not mean choosing to remain single forever. It doesn't mean giving up on marriage.*

Moreover, we can use our singleness as an excuse for many of our problems... 'It's not my fault I'm late – it was the bus'. Sometimes, we can even use our singleness to avoid confronting our issues, relying on the belief that there is no need to deal with them until *He* comes along.

Choosing to ride towards our destiny is more involved. Firstly, it's a dynamic thing. It means continually and actively making decisions that propel us forward. It means choosing over and over again to push the pedals up and down and up and down and up and down.

Riding also means we choose to take responsibility for our own lives and journeys. It means facing our issues, our insecurities and our questions and persevering on the journey despite them. But don't forget, riding is not without its rewards. We will reach our destination fitter, healthier and probably more fulfilled than if we had just waited for the bus.

Choosing to ride does not mean choosing to remain single forever. It doesn't mean giving up on marriage. It simply means that we will no longer be defined by our singleness or let life pass us by while we wait for a man to come along. It means that instead of waiting for someone else to pick us up and take us on towards our future, we will take steps to actively move in that direction ourselves. Who knows, maybe one day we'll be riding along and glance to the left and find that someone is cycling along beside us? What better way to meet someone – than to know that they are already heading in the same direction as you?

This book is about how to ride your bike...

This book is about how to ride your bike, rather than just waiting around for however long, marking time, hoping a bus will come. There are some tips and tricks I have learned along the way, a couple of myths that I've realized lots of us have been believing, some 'How To's' and a couple of chapters that tackle some of the things that no one really likes talking about.

Myth No. 1:

Marriage is a *Right*

I have met girls who feel they have been ripped off. They believe that God has let them down. He hasn't come through for them in the marriage department. When they signed on to be a Christian, Jesus promised them an abundant life and their interpretation of *abundance* included a husband. When the husband didn't arrive on the scene straight away (or even one, two or three years later) they began to question God and became increasingly disillusioned with the whole thing.

Now, it's common knowledge that Christians tend to get married quite young - usually in their early 20s and sometimes even their late teens (and I think we all have our own theories as to *why* this is...) Interestingly, this is in total contrast to the culture that we live in, where the average marriage age is around 28 years for women and 30 years for men and it's now estimated that up to 25% of people won't ever get married. Anyway, the point is, because of the trend for Christians to marry young, an expectation has developed within the church that marriage is something that will definitely happen for all of us and it will most probably take place in our early twenties.

However, just because marriage is common doesn't mean that it is therefore something we are *entitled* to. Nowhere in the Bible does it say that life in Christ will provide us with everything we want and desire at exactly the time that we would like it to happen. (Encouragingly though, the Bible *does* reveal that we serve an incredibly generous God who cares very much about our lives, but this still doesn't make marriage something we have the *right* to.)

Furthermore, marriage isn't something that we *deserve*. It is very dangerous to view marriage as something that is deserved, because that would then mean that people who aren't married are

Marriage isn't something that we deserve

somehow less *deserving* of a partner. There can be an implication that those who aren't married are less worthy and less valuable than their married peers. History tells us that this is not the case. (Just think of Mother Teresa who was undeniably one of the most influential and 'successful' Christians to ever live, and she never married.)

Another issue with believing that marriage is *deserved* is that there is a temptation to draw comparisons with others. Particularly when couples get married very young, it's easy to think, 'Oh but I deserve to get married so much more. I've been waiting for years. I'm so much more mature and ready for marriage than they are...' It's always good to remember that marriage is not an indicator of spiritual or emotional maturity. If we approach marriage as something we are entitled to or deserve, we will naturally begin to feel that God has neglected us or is punishing us if He has not *provided* a husband. And if we don't end up blaming God, we will probably end up turning the blame onto ourselves and become overly critical, focussing on  all of the possible reasons why we don't *deserve* to get married. (*I'm too fat, too loud, too quiet, too selfish, too nerdy...*)

Another downfall to viewing marriage as a *right* is that there is a tendency to think that we can 'earn' marriage or work our way towards it. You know that this is a problem for you when you start thinking, 'If I just (fill in the blank: dress nicer, speak more, speak less, lose weight, do more ministry), someone will be sure to fall in love with me'.

If we want a healthy view of marriage we must see it as a precious gift. Like all of God's gifts it isn't given to us because we *deserve* it. If this were the case we wouldn't be given anything, because we don't really *deserve* anything from God. As it is, everything we have, our very lives have been *given* to us from His generous heart. God doesn't love you less if he hasn't given you a partner with whom to share your life.

If we consider marriage as a gift, we will be surprised and delighted if God brings someone along and we will enter into marriage thankful for the blessing that has been given to us. Likewise, in the period of time before possible marriage there will be less temptation to blame God or ourselves and we will be freed from 'working' for something that is (on the whole) out of our control. There is such freedom awaiting those who stop believing marriage is something they deserve.

Something to think about:

Have you ever considered the effect that living in a consumer culture has had on you and your views of marriage? Is marriage just another box that you want to tick in order to fulfil the list of things that our culture says you should have by the time you are a certain age? Are you frustrated because although you have an iphone, a sweet car, a satisfying job and a fulfilling ministry, the 'Husband' box remains unticked? I wonder if our culture has lost the understanding of what a true **gift** is, and instead we expect to get what we want, when we want it.

'Be patient toward all that is unsolved in your heart and try to love the questions themselves. Do not now seek the answers, which cannot be given you because you would not be able to live them. Live your questions now, and perhaps even without knowing it, you will live along some distant day into your answers.'

- Rainer Maria Rilke

Not to *scare* you
but you should probably know...

We're not alone on earth. Ok, so it's not like the movies and there are no aliens, but we *are* involved in a giant spiritual battle. Thankfully, we're on the winning side. (If you're unsure about this, try reading through the book of Revelation - it lays things out pretty clearly.) The thing is, the enemy camp doesn't play fair. Satan will use whatever he can get his hands on to sideline you and make you doubt who you are and who God is and what the heck He is doing in your life. He will go after your weak spot and delight in trying to distort reality.

In saying this, please don't take me to mean that you are single because the enemy is preventing you from meeting the love of your life. What I am saying is that if getting married is something that is important to you, it is likely that the enemy will attempt to distort your views on it and use it as something that will pull you away from God. His main strategy is to whisper lies to you. He'll say things like...

No one will ever love you. You're unlovable.
God has failed you. It's time to do things on your own.
You're single because God is punishing you.
You're not as effective in ministry as a married couple would be.
You had your chance and you screwed it up. You'll be alone forever.
Play the damsel role and your hero will come to rescue you.
No one will want you because you're... (fill in the blank: not a virgin, too ugly, have anxiety problems, too boring, suffer from depression...)
There are no good Christian guys left. You should look for one outside the church.

There is no end to the lies that he will try to get you to believe about yourself. The goal is to disarm you, to get you to doubt God and to make you believe that you're not a loved, valuable and effective child in God's Kingdom. If he can get you to believe those lies about yourself, then you're not too much of a threat to his plans. In John 10:10 Jesus says that the enemy comes to steal, kill and destroy. I believe that this means that he attempts to steal our identity, kill our dreams and destroy our hope. So what can we do about this?

How can we tell the difference between lies and legitimate thoughts?

Firstly, we need to recognize that we're all going to have moments when we question and doubt and wrestle with things that are deep and painful. There will inevitably be moments for all of us when our emotions and feelings seem to overtake our logical thought.

(*They say* that's part of being female; personally I think it happens to everyone.) I remember many times when I've said things like, 'I *know* that I'm loved, but right now I don't *feel* loved,' or 'I *know* that God is meant to be good, but right now I am SO angry at Him'.

Some people would tell you that it's wrong to think these things or to question God like that, but a wise man that I knew gave me a different perspective. He said that the issues we face, the questions, the doubts, and the fears about who we are and what is going on in our lives are not what's important. What's important is whether, as we grapple with those things, we choose to walk *towards* God or *away* from Him.

> *The enemy will tell you lies with the intention of drawing you away from God.*

The enemy will tell you lies with the intention of drawing you away from God. It's our choice what we do with the lies that are whispered. If you are hearing lies that are bringing you down, the best thing you can do is to take them to God. Be honest with Him. Say, 'This is what I am feeling right now. What do you have to say to me about that?' Ask Him to shine His light into your mind, to draw out the truth and remove the lies.

A while ago, I had to put this into practice. I was having a bit of a blue day. I liked a boy and he didn't like me back. And in my head a voice started saying 'Of course he doesn't like you back. Same old story. No one you like ever likes you, blah, blah, blah…' (In the past, I have just agreed with the voice and let it ruin my day or week!) That morning though, I had been singing a song to God that had the line in it, 'You make all things work together for my good'. And so I went to God and I asked Him... 'How *are* you making this work for good? Because right now it doesn't feel good. It hurts.'

I learned a lot from His response.

He said that I was looking at the situation from my own perspective, my earthly, very human perspective and that He actually saw things differently. He invited me to come and look at things through His eyes. And as I began to look at things from His perspective (the heavenly one) I realized that what I was seeing as rejection was actually God's protection. He went on to show me how He saw a whole lot of things that have happened in my past, what His plan had been through them and where He had been working in them.

I guess the lesson that I learned was that we all need to continually align our perspective with God's perspective and let Him tell us what is truth and what is lies.

10 things

that we should all
stop believing

1. I will be happy, fulfilled, secure and whole when I am married

2. All the good Christian guys have been taken

3. Single women are less effective in ministry than married couples

4. True happiness and singleness are mutually exclusive

5. I am a failure as a woman because I am not married

6. Other people think I am a failure because I'm not married

7. I won't be lonely when I am married

8. When I get married I'll know what to do with the rest of my life

9. When I'm married I won't have any issues with lust or temptation

10. The best years of my life are being wasted

Myth No. 2:

'I'm a damsel in *distress*'

When I was in Year 10 our whole year level had to take a self-defence class. The only thing I can remember from it was that they taught us that if we were being attacked or threatened we should start screaming at the top of our lungs, 'I am not a victim… I am not a victim… I am not a victim!'

I thought it was weird at the time, and I still think it's a pretty strange thing to do. Can you imagine running through the streets screaming, 'I am not a victim'? People would look at you with a sympathetic nod of agreement – you're not a victim, you're a lunatic! Anyway, the instructors told us that the theory was, most people who are assaulted don't tend to scream or defend themselves because they're too focussed on the person attacking them. Therefore if you start yelling, 'I am not a victim' the attacker realizes that you are going to put up a fight and they are less likely to continue their assault. Although in shock, you remind yourself that you don't have to be a victim to their attack. Thankfully I've never had to put my self-defence training into practice (except for the occasional sock wrestling episode when I've found the yell-scream-kick-wriggle manoeuvre that they taught us quite useful).

It has made me wonder though, how many of us see ourselves as *victims* to the *monster* of singleness. Do we see singleness as an affliction that we must suffer through? Is it a period of time and a circumstance that is out of our control? Have we become the princess tragically stranded in her white tower waiting to be rescued by her Prince Charming? Popular culture would answer with a resounding 'Yes', given the number of box office hit romantic comedies that have been made to that formula. Now, it must be said – I love romcoms as much as the next girl, and all of my Top Five movies would probably fall into that category, but I think it is important that we all question how much the view of love and romance portrayed in these films has influenced the way we view our own journey of singleness.

How many of us see ourselves as victims to the monster of singleness?

It's interesting to consider how our generation ended up here, given that many of our mothers and grandmothers fought fiercely for women's rights and to give women an identity apart from the men they married. They made it possible for women to vote, to buy houses, to own businesses, to travel the world on their own... and yet somehow many of us have reverted back to this view that single women (ourselves included) need to be *rescued* from our singleness.

There are several assumptions tied up in this type of thinking. The first is that *singleness is a bad thing*. The very concept of being rescued implies that you are in an undesirable situation in the first place. The second assumption is that you are a *helpless victim of your circumstances*, and that the only way for your circumstances to change is for you to be rescued by a man.

A consequence of thinking like this is that we are in great danger of missing out on the things that we are meant to be doing in the present season because we see ourselves as *passive victims* rather than *active participants* in our lives. If we see ourselves as victims to singleness, we will view the period of time that we are single, however long or short, as something that must be overcome and we may not recognize that now is a season of significance and importance in our lives.

How we see ourselves will determine how we live

The truth is, how we see ourselves will determine how we live, what choices we make and how effectively God can work in and through our lives. It's back to the question of whether we are going to wait at the bus stop, or jump on our bikes and ride?

So here it is. I think maybe it's time we started yelling, 'I am not a victim!' at the top of our lungs, because I, for one, refuse to see myself (or let others see me) as a helpless victim to singleness. I am not going to live my life in a tower locked away from the world waiting for my *real life* to begin when the Prince comes to rescue me.

How to:

Keep smiling for an **entire** wedding

Weddings are generally acknowledged to be the one of the most traumatic experiences in a single girl's life. There's the awkward conversations, the wobbly walk from the car in too-high heels without an arm to hang on to, there's the shame of being seated on the 'leftovers' table, the disappointment of being alone in your seat whilst 'everyone else' is dancing with their partners, not to mention the embarrassing tradition of being lined up with all of the other single girls and having a bouquet thrown at you.

But here's the wrap. It's not about us. Not one tiny bit. And that's what we all need to focus on when we are attending our umpteenth wedding. It's about the bride and the groom (who, if you recall, are probably good friends or even family members of ours.) And it's about celebrating with them. It's about coming alongside them and sharing in their joy. *Even if it costs us.*

1. Perspective

The first tip is to remember to bring our *perspective* with us. Remembering that it's not about us, it's not our day and that it's not an excuse for a pity party is a good start. It can also be helpful to reflect that for the vast majority of weddings we attend, we don't actually want to be marrying the groom, and so there is not much reason to be upset that we're not the ones getting married that day. When we think about it that way, it is a lot easier to be genuinely joyful for the couple getting married.

'Remember to bring your perspective with you'

2. Get ready with a friend

I've found this is good in a few ways. Firstly, you can get outfit/hair/makeup advice and help from each other and pool your resources (eg: not have to buy a new outfit for each wedding, but swap and share clothes, accessories and makeup). Secondly, it's usually fun and often very helpful in that there is someone to laugh with you when you burn your forehead with the curling iron or to let you know that you've put your dress on inside out and to remind you that it's not the end of the world if your shoes don't quite match your dress. Thirdly, it means that you don't have to arrive at the wedding on your own or search awkwardly for a seat next to someone you know. Finally, it's good for the environment to carpool. ☺

3. Look nice

As women, we all approach getting *dressed up* differently. Some of us love it. Some of us loathe it. And we all have different views on what 'looking nice' actually means. So, with absolutely no judgement on whether you wear makeup or not, whether you like to wear dresses or enjoy wearing jeans, this is why I choose to look nice at weddings...

Weddings stand out to me as one of the few traditional events left in our culture that people still get *dressed up* for. When I get dressed up (this is obviously for a formal wedding), I feel as if I am in a small way honoring the bride and groom, by showing them that I feel it is an important and worthwhile occasion.

I've heard women ask why they would bother dressing up or looking nice for a wedding if they know there's 'not going to be anyone there to impress'. I don't think our motivation for looking nice should be that we want to impress men or catch their attention. However, without going into the intricacies of whether this is *right* or *wrong*, I've found that I feel better about myself when I look nice. And, as weddings are often a place where us single girls can begin to get a wee bit down about *not* being with someone, knowing that I look nice and feeling good about myself has often proven to be a good thing.

4. Be organized

There was this one time when all of my friends, or so it seemed to me, had planned to do things with their partners in the gap between wedding and reception, and I found myself stuck with a two hour break and a mind that was full to bursting with lonely, 'woe-is-me' thoughts. I bought a magazine and sat in a café feeling like I was the loneliest person in the world, determined to be miserable and dwell on how *unfair* my life was. Once I got to the reception, I realized that there had been plenty of people that I could have hung out with, it was just that I hadn't been organized enough to actually make plans with any of them. Since then, I've decided to *plan* what I am going to do in the space between the wedding and reception. Even if that means planning to spend time on my own, the fact that it is an intentional decision and not just something I have been forced into seems to make it that much easier to swallow.

5. Don't drink too much

I don't want to labor this point, but drinking as a way to escape feelings of loneliness or insecurity is not really a helpful solution and in the long-term is likely to make things worse.

6. Don't drive home on your own

Again, this is one that is quite subjective – some of us enjoy a solitary drive, others find it achingly lonely. I generally enjoy driving on my own, but when it comes to weddings I've found I like to debrief afterwards and so driving home with someone or a group of someones is fun and helpful and usually prevents me from dwelling too much on any post-wedding blues that may creep into my mind.

'Father God is neither care-less nor cause-less with how he spends our lives.' [1]

- Alicia Britt Chole

[1] Chole, Alicia Britt, 2006, *Anonymous*, Thomas Nelson, Tennessee.

Myth No. 3:

'A man will **complete** me'

There is a frequently quoted scene from the movie 'Liar Liar' when the son, Max tells his Dad that his teacher said that 'beauty is on the inside'. Fletcher, the father, replies, 'That's just something ugly people say'. It's a statement that has been repeated many times in popular culture, with different variations, thankfully in a joking sense most of the time! When I was reflecting on the two statements though, I realized just how powerful the second comment is as it completely undermines the first. If someone said to me, 'Your beauty is on the inside,' and I had already heard 'That's just something ugly people say', I could quite easily assume that they were implying that I was ugly and fail to recognize their statement as a legitimate compliment. This has made wonder how many of us have heard the statement,

'Jesus is enough for you', and heard a responding comment in our heads that goes something like, 'That's just what they tell you when you're single'? We disarm the first statement by questioning the intentions of people who say it. Rather than accepting it as a serious statement that could convict and empower us, 'Jesus is enough for you' becomes a cliché that we sing in church, but do not truly embrace in our lives.

There was a period in my life where I would become frustrated by people who made statements like, 'Jesus is more than enough', or 'Let Jesus be your husband'. I would look at them and (often) they had Jesus *and* a husband and I would self-righteously think, 'Well, if Jesus was all you needed, why did you get married? You're just saying that to make me feel better.' It wasn't very generous of me or very logical, but that was where I was at the time.

I've found that it is a lot easier to disregard statements that challenge me even if they are true, than it is to actually face them and wrestle with them. Eventually, I chose to be honest with myself and with God and began to ask some tough questions. 'If I don't feel that Jesus is enough for me, why is that?'

Am I the problem?
Is Jesus the problem?
Was Jesus lying when He said he came to give life to the full?
Or are my expectations of life unrealistic?
Is there more of Jesus that I am not experiencing?

Looking back now, it has been such a powerful experience to truly consider what it means for Jesus to be *enough* in my life. Painful? Yes. Humbling? Of course. Worthwhile? Without a doubt. It's been valuable in many ways and has effectively realigned my whole life, not just in how I view singleness and marriage. I've found that there is a safety and freedom in knowing *for sure* that Jesus is enough. I can rest in the knowledge that Jesus will be enough for me, and the thought of never getting married or being single for a long time doesn't have the same power to instil fear into my core like it used to.

Overall, I am a lot less tempted to approach marriage with unfair expectations of my husband that he should fulfil me, complete me or be everything that I need in life. In saying that, God hasn't taken away my *desire* for a husband, but now I have an understanding that I am a whole and fulfilled person even without one.

I understand that this is a tough journey to take and I don't want to create false expectations. Even when you actually believe from the bottom of your heart that Jesus completes you, you're still going to encounter loneliness and pain and longing. That's the reality of life I'm afraid. But can I encourage you to consider for yourself whether you think Jesus *is* enough in your life? Or are you waiting for a man to come along to *complete* you?

....

Note: Just in case you were thinking that I am some saint who is totally perfect and never complains about not being married, let me set the record straight. I still have freakouts and breakdowns and crack-it moments about being single. And I think it's ok to have *moments*. It's just that we need to remember to only *visit* that place, but never actually pitch our tent and *live* there.

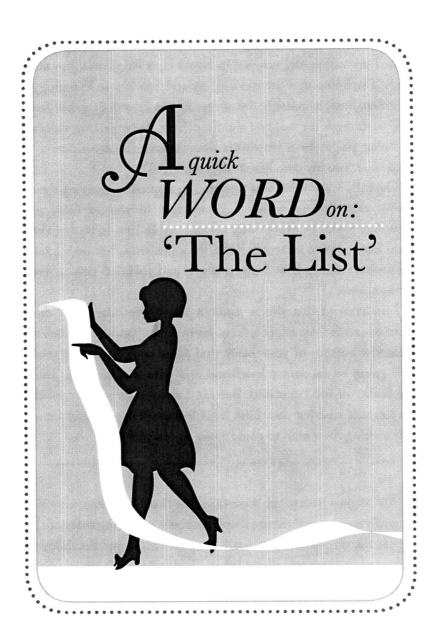

A _quick_ _WORD_ _on:_ 'The List'

A long time ago, I wrote a list. A list of all of the qualities I wanted in a husband. For me it was partly to help me *find* the right guy, and partly to stop me from marrying any guy who came along.

I'm still not sure if I think it's a good idea or not. It seems to be quite a divisive topic really. My sister swears by the list. Hers was massively long and she is now married to a guy who ticks all of the boxes. I heard of a guy whose list was so specific it even had *skinny ankles* on it, and he married a girl with possibly the skinniest ankles ever. Other people have told me that lists are a bad idea because they limit God or because although we know what we want we don't really know what we *need*.

Anyway, whether having a guy-list is a good thing or a bad thing is not really my point right now. I guess the point I want to get to is that we all have certain expectations about who it is that we would like to be with and what they should be like.

> We all have certain expectations about who it is that we want to be with and what they will be like.

A couple of years ago I was having a read through my list with a friend and she challenged me that if I had a list of qualities I wanted in a man, did I have a list of qualities that I was aspiring to live up to also? Ouch.

It's good to have *standard*s. For sure. It's also good to be thinking and praying about what you would be looking for in a potential partner. But we also need to ask ourselves, 'In this season of life, am I growing and developing? Am I setting expectations and goals and working towards them?' Or am I writing down a list of things that I want in a man and yet not bothering to develop my own character?

I hate to admit this, but there are girls who are so focussed on what they want in a guy, and they spend so much time fantasising about how amazing *he* will be, they never actually look at their own life or examine their own heart and character.

After my friend's challenge, I decided to write a list. A Taryn-list. I prayed into it and took my time drafting it up. I was working at a fashion store at the time and I spent hours standing at the counter pretending to fill in stock orders when really I was taking stock of my own life. I wrote it as a prophetic declaration of who I wanted to be. I've found it to be powerful speaking things out as declarations because it helps me to believe them and start living up to them. I read over it fairly regularly and it reminds me of who I am becoming and sets a standard to which I aspire to live my life.

It's a couple of pages long, and covers lots of different areas of my life, but here are a few excerpts so you can get what I'm talking about:

'I am a woman who is confidently herself all of the time. My behavior is not defined by the behavior, standards, or expectations of those around me, although I am always sensitive to the environment I am in.'

'I am a woman who celebrates her body. I care for it, but I do not obsess over it. I enjoy its unique features and recognize that beauty lies in the difference. I enjoy the contrasts but I never compare.'

'I am a woman who is extravagantly generous, and yet has clearly defined boundaries.'

'I am a woman who approaches confrontation confidently, with a goal of mutual understanding and resolution.'

'I do not take offence easily. I approach criticism objectively, not defensively and take personal criticism to God, with an open heart asking Him to reveal the truth and a relevant plan of action.'

'I am a woman of my word. When I say I'll do something, I will do it. I am faithful and reliable. I respect and honor indiscriminately.'

I'd encourage you to write your own list. It may just have a few points. It may be ten pages long. Pray about it. Think about it. Take your time working out who you are becoming and what values you want to aspire to in your life.

Myth No. 4:

'If I was married I wouldn't be lonely'

I have heard it said that alone we enter this world and alone we will leave it. It does seem like quite a gloomy thought, but it is in many ways profoundly true. As humans we can be *with* people and we can grow very close to people, but we are all still unchangeably individual. Ruth Haley Barton summarises this notion really well in her book 'Longing for More':

'In one sense *we are all single*! Married or not, we all stand alone before God, accountable to him and to him alone for the expenditure of our life and love and spiritual service.' [2]

It's fair to say that you will probably not encounter *as much* loneliness when you are married (simply because you will not be on your own as much). However, let's be clear about this: A husband will

[2] Barton, RH, 2007, *Longing for More*, Intervarsity Press, London.

not understand everything about you. No man (or woman for that matter) will ever *get* everything that you feel or need to express. A husband won't always know what to say or how to say it, and he won't always be there for you at every moment of every day. If you are waiting for a husband to take away your basic human aloneness you will continue to wait even when you are married.

We're all going to encounter moments of loneliness and 'loserishness'. And it is ok to feel those things occasionally. The problem lies in how we deal with those emotions when we feel them. So often we dwell on them. We think, 'If only I had a boyfriend / husband, I would never be lonely... I would never have boring Saturday nights... I'd never feel like a loner...' And we meditate on those thoughts. We eat chocolate. We buy expensive things to distract ourselves. We complain to anyone who'll listen. It's not too long before a lonely moment becomes a lonely week, becomes a lonely month, becomes an ocean of loneliness that threatens to swallow our whole lives.

> *We're all going to encounter moments of loneliness and loserishness.*

Have you ever had an 'I am lonely' that became an 'I am SO lonely' that grew into an 'I am the loneliest person in the world', that then turned into an, 'Even if I go to that party everyone else will have a partner and I'll be the only single person and I'll just feel even more lonely so I won't go at all,' experience?

Something that starts as a thought escalates to the point where it actually significantly affects our behavior and the way we choose to live. In some ways the 'I am lonely' becomes a self-fulfilling prophecy, because it leads us to the point where we choose not to go to the party and be with other people which would possibly have alleviated our initial loneliness, or at the very least diverted us from those thoughts.

It's important to consider what we are thinking about...

It's true that we walk towards what we fix our eyes on and if what we fix our eyes on is our aloneness, we will become consumed by it. It's not that we need to *distract* ourselves from our circumstances – but it's important to consider what it is we are thinking about the most and what sort of things we are telling ourselves. If we think, 'I am so alone. I am so alone...' then we will believe that we are alone. If we think, 'I am a woman who is content in her circumstance and pursuing God and His destiny for my life', we will most likely believe that too. I'm not saying that we can just *psych* ourselves out of ever feeling lonely again. BUT what we *choose* to do with those lonely thoughts will make a difference to how we feel and live.

How to: Overcome Loneliness

Everyone knows that too many Saturday nights home alone are going to bring anyone down. It's never a fun feeling at 5pm on a Saturday realising that your housemate is away for the weekend, your bestie is hanging with her husband, your sister is looking after her kids, even your parents are at a party and you've got no plans. When it comes to loneliness, prevention is absolutely the best cure. We may not be able to stamp it out completely, but we can all make choices that will minimise the amount of time we spend sulking on the couch eating chocolate cookies and watching our favorite chick-flick for the millionth time. Here's my top few...

Be Organized

Organization does not come naturally to me, but I've found that it totally pays to plan out my weekends in advance. If I realize a few days ahead that I have nothing to do on a Saturday night then I have time to organize something and a higher chance of finding people to hang out with and a movie, restaurant or concert that isn't already booked out. Oftentimes we become discouraged, rejected and consequently lonely when we call people up on the day and they already have plans. Being organized prevents this from happening.

Another thing I've found helpful is to actually *schedule* in nights at home on my own. When you have *chosen* to spend the night in, it feels very different than being *forced* into it because no one is available to hang out with you. It can be freeing and restorative to choose to be on your own and to really enjoy your own company.

Be the proactive one

Have you ever seen an event, concert, exhibition, market or festival advertized and lamented that you've got no one to go with? Chances are you *do* have many people in your life who would love to go to it too, it's just that everyone seems to expect everyone else to organize the group and not many people actually do the proactive thing and invite others along.

I find that it can be the same with meeting men. There is a consistent complaint amongst single girls of, 'I just never meet new guys' and yet very few of them are willing to actually organize themselves (and their friends) to be in a position where they *may* meet new people. A good way to think about it is to ask yourself, 'What would I like my friends to do for me?' and then be that friend for them. This may mean you become the one who looks in the newspaper for the latest events to go to and messages everyone else the details. You may be the one who is always having BBQs and movie nights. I guarantee the rest of your friends will thank you for it.

Get yourself a sponsor

Ok, so this may sound weird, but hear me out. Something that I have realized is that when I am feeling lonely I am also generally feeling trapped in that loneliness. And it feels like there are only two types of people with whom to share and neither option is very appealing...

The ones who *get it* are the other single girls. The problem with them is that I often end up more discouraged than when I started because instead of lifting each other up we tend to complain and whinge and our collective loneliness can descend into bitterness. The alternative is to share with married friends. And the problem there is that we feel that they no longer truly *get it*. And when people respond to our heart cry with clichés that don't validate or encourage, we can be left feeling misunderstood.

So, what to do? My suggestion is to word up a friend (married or not) who agrees to be your 'sponsor'. Talk to them about the role that you would like them to play in your life. Explain that you need someone who will be compassionate and hear you out. Someone who agrees not to answer everything you say with a Bible verse or an inspirational quote. Someone who, at the end of your vent, will pick you up, throw you back on your bike and remind you of the direction in which you're heading. Returning to the opening illustration, every now and then we will all get tired of riding, our muscles will get sore, we may take a fall or even be hit by a truck. It's at these moments that we need someone who knows God, knows our journey, knows us, and knows where we are heading. Someone who can compassionately bandage us up, and send us back on our way.

Another thing to note on this point is that there are few things less attractive than someone who is consistently complaining about their singleness. It is for this reason that we all need to make sure we intentionally choose the people who we speak with about it and not scatter the deep stories of our heart around to anyone who will listen.

God time

This is pretty simple. When I am actively pursuing my relationship with God (and I mean *actively* pursuing) not just showing up each week at church and praying every now and then, but actually investing my time and energy into my relationship with Jesus, I find that the husband flutters (that's what my old housemate and I used to call them) aren't nearly so bad. And sometimes I even forget them altogether.

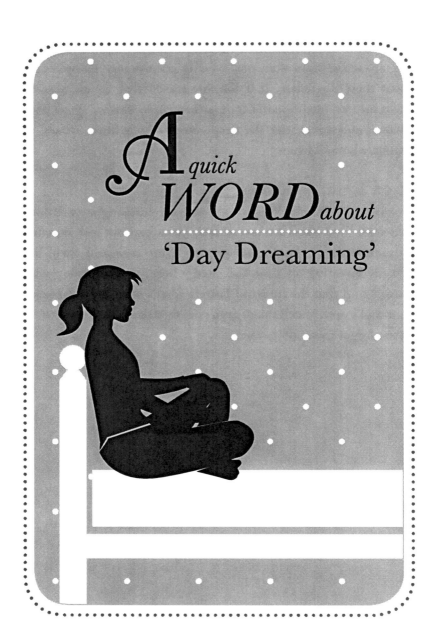

A quick **WORD** *about* 'Day Dreaming'

When I was about 14 one of my friends and I started a secret scrapbook. One of us would make an entry and then conspiratorially give it to the other for a few weeks and then we'd swap it back. We wrote letters to each other, we made collages about our jobs, compiled our dreams and wrote about our future plans. We even charted all of the love triangles that had happened in our youth group over the years. That entry became quite a complicated page! Another one of the things that we used to do was to make up *Episodes* for each other – stories of how the other was going to fall in love. Generally they involved being rescued by our current crush from a dramatic life or death scenario and living happily, ever after. It was fun and fairly harmless and has provided us great entertainment now as we look back over the stories.

Reflecting on our scrapbook though, makes me wonder – how many of us are still making up *Episodes* in our heads? Are we dreaming and imagining how and when and with whom we'll fall in love? Replacing the face of the *hero* with whoever we are secretly admiring?

A few years ago, the Lord really convicted me about my thought life and what I was spending most of my time thinking about. I realized that I was spending a good deal of my time dreaming and fantasizing about falling in love. God spoke to me really clearly through a verse in Proverbs where it says, 'Hope deferred makes the heart sick, but a longing fulfilled is a tree of life.' (Proverbs 13:12) What I felt God was telling me was that by spending so much time fantasising about falling in love I was putting a dispro-portionate amount of hope into something that wasn't Him. And as a consequence my heart was starting to feel sick, (down, lonely, despondent), because each time I had made up an *Episode* in my head and it hadn't *come true* there was a sense of disappointment.

'Hope deferred makes the heart sick...'

In sharing this, I don't believe that it is wrong to hope to get married. And it's natural to imagine how and when this could happen. But we must be careful *how much* time we give to these thoughts. It's very easy to slip into an imaginary world only to find ourselves returning to a disappointing reality. We must also be aware that the thought patterns we develop now will continue on into the future and into any future relationship. It won't be as simple as saying to ourselves, 'Well, now that I'm married there is no need to fantasise any-more', because our minds will natu-rally continue to do the things that we've trained them to do.

I was talking to a friend once about this and we began to wonder what would happen if we replaced all of the time that we currently spend thinking and fan-tasizing about our *happily ever after*, thinking about God, dream-ing with God, coming up with new ideas or stories or artworks...

'I will consider all your works
and meditate on all your mighty deeds.'

Psalm 77:12

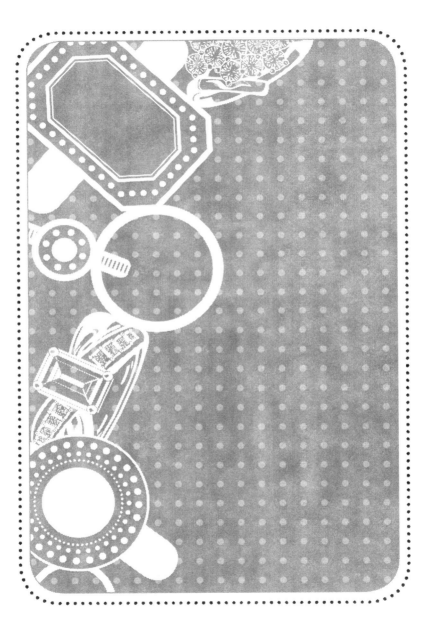

Myth No. 5:

'The grass is **greener** on the married side'

One day I was walking along a trail that ran through a farm and I saw a really peculiar thing. There were several goats in the paddock that ran alongside the path and even though they had a large grazing area with lovely luscious grass, all of them had their heads wedged under the fence and they were nibbling the grass on the edge of the walking track. It was such a classic example of the old saying, 'The grass is greener on the other side'. What looked really funny was when they tried to pull their heads back into their own paddock they kept getting tangled in the fence.

I think many of us believe that the grass is greener on the *married* side. Married people have companionship. They have fun dates. They have someone to laugh with, to share secrets with, someone to snuggle up with at night. No one will deny that married grass can be undoubtedly green. But here's the thing, although it may be green, it's not necessarily greener – just a different shade of green. Because the reality is, the grass is only green where you water it.

'The grass is only green where you water it'

There are marriages where the grass is thriving and lush; there are also marriages where the grass is shrivelled and brown. In the same way there are single people who have watered their lives and have a thriving crop and others whose lives resemble barren fields. Our satisfaction with our own lives has a lot more to do with whether we are caring for our own paddock, than it has to do with whether we are married or not. It's easy to claim we're dissatisfied with our lives because we're *not* married, or to believe that our lives would be better if we *were* married. We all need to consider whether our singleness is the *real* reason for our dissatisfaction, or if there are actually deeper issues concerning who we are and what our lives consist of that are causing our unrest.

I was praying with a friend and afterwards she shared with me that she felt that the Lord has given me a whole lot of seeds and that this is the season I need to be planting them. She explained that for some of these things, now will be the *only* time that I have to plant and that the opportunities I have now won't come around again. She stressed the importance of truly embracing and being content in the season that I am currently in.

If you are single, it's more than likely that this is God's plan for your life right now and there is no doubt that he has filled your pockets with seeds and is hoping that you will sow them in the paddock that He has you in. If you are standing at the fence staring at married grass on the other side, chances are you won't be planting your seeds or watering your paddock and you will be potentially missing some incredible opportunities that may only come around once.

So it's time to take a look into your pockets and discover what surprises God has hidden in there - what seeds he has ready for you to cultivate in your life.

We
are *all* a
work **in**
progress

Note: As I said at the beginning, this book isn't about 'preparing' for a husband, so I want to give you a little explanation as to why I have included this chapter. I think it would be fair to say that many of us have a desire to be married, and I firmly believe that we can hold onto this desire, whilst still finding contentment and joy in singleness. And because of this desire I think it's important, every now and then, (can I really stress the *every now and then* part – not every day), to consider if there is anything on our part that could be holding us back from entering into a relationship or be detrimental if we were to be in one.

There are two things that you must remember as you read this chapter...

Number 1 We are loved by God. Now. Today. Passionately. Without exception. Just as we are.

Number 2 We are also being perfected by Him. Meaning that we are not perfect. Not yet anyway.

And as we walk through life we must hold these two things in tension – we're fully loved and accepted *and* Christ is wanting to work in us, change and grow us; crafting us more into His image.

There are many reasons why we are single: by choice, because of timing, circumstances, God's plan and mysterious way of working... and there is also the possibility that there are areas in our lives that are actually hindering us from entering into a relationship.

This could look like many things. It may be baggage from a past relationship or sexual experience. Sometimes things happen in life that are out of our control: abuse, dysfunctional family relationships, mental illness. And sometimes, we've made decisions that have led us down unhealthy paths.

> *If we hide things away in darkness, over time they will manifest themselves in our behavior, in our attitudes, and in the way that we relate to others.*

In no way would I suggest that these things are *the* reason that we are single. However, we all need to work *with* God in our lives and part of our responsibility is to come to Him with the things that we are burdened by and ask for Him to take us on a journey towards healing. This is not always a simple process, as each of our lives are made up of many complex layers. Even when we enter a place of healing and wholeness, the consequences of things that have occurred in our past may remain and our task is to learn how to live with those things. The question is not, 'Are we completely healed and therefore ready to be used by God in life?' The question is more along the lines of, 'Are we being honest about who we are and what we are going through and choosing to walk *with* God on a journey towards healing?'

If we hide things away in darkness, over time they will manifest themselves in our behavior, in our attitudes, and in the way that we relate to others. Unless we expose things to God's light, we will carry them with us into *every* relationship we enter, not just romantic relationships.

I find it encouraging that this is not a journey we have to do on our own. There is counselling and prayer ministry, mentors and pastors who are willing to walk with us, and often one of the greatest things in life can be the prayer and support of a close friend.

A little while ago a married friend of mine confronted me about an issue in my life that she felt would be detrimental if I was to enter into a relationship in the future. It wasn't the nicest feeling to start with, but I listened to what she said and prayed about it and realized that there was truth in what she said and I needed to alter some of my behaviors.

If you're not sure where to start, maybe talk to a trusted friend and ask them if they feel that there are any issues or areas in your life that may be a concern in future relationships. It's a brave move, and you have to be prepared to hear the hard truth from them when they give you an answer.

It's not often pleasant to face issues and begin to work through them. But it is *so* satisfying to know that we no longer have to be held captive by them and that our God is a God who is willing to walk the journey with us, and who always has a plan for restoration.

So this is the chapter that I least wanted to write. Because there's something that us good Christian girls don't seem to talk very much about. Oh, I know we talk about sex, probably more with our unchurched friends than our churchies if we're honest about it. But not many people seem to talk much about the *not having* part.

How do you *not have* sex? Most of us are at an age where we would be classified as sexually mature adults. Now, I'm not sure if I believe all the research about having an age at which you *sexually peak* because from what I've heard you can have great sex at any age. However, science says that our 20s/30s are probably the age where we have the most hormones running around our bodies that we're ever going to have. So what do we do with all of the *butterflies* inside when they don't have anywhere to go? And, often more importantly than the actual *sex* thing, is the issue of physical intimacy - kissing, snuggling and all that hand holding that we feel we're missing out on.

This journey is complicated by the fact that as Christian women we have to navigate our way through a culture where, although it's not unusual for women in their 20s and 30s to be single, it is highly unusual for them to not be sexually active. In the world in which we live, anyone who is over the age of 18 and not sexually active is a complete anomaly. And so many of us find that our chosen road is not really an option that the world recognizes, and yet it isn't something that is, on the whole, discussed or supported within the church either. Many churches have got to the place where they are talking about how to walk in purity within dating relationships (which is great), but it seems that we find it a lot harder to admit that the same issues can be difficult and challenging for singles too.

I'm not going to give you the answers to this one. To be honest, I can't say I've fully figured it out just yet. However, there are a few things that I have found to be helpful for me, and I've listed them below. What I will say is: *this is something that we need to start talking about.*

Any issue will seem huge and insurmountable if you think you're the only one struggling with it. And living as a sexual being without having sex is the same. If you feel like you're the only single girl who ever finds it difficult, or who ever faces temptation in this area, you need to know you're not alone. It is such a relief to know that others are journeying through the same issue. When we share our struggles with each other, we are then empowered to pray for and support each other and work out ways that we can keep each other accountable.

There's no need to go and tell the world about your struggles, but just start by talking to a few of your trusted girlfriends. Maybe talk to some older women and ask them what they have learned along the way. Look at the Bible together and see if you can find anything that relates – you may be surprised by what you find.

Things that I find helpful to keep the butterflies at bay:

Work out your triggers:

So I've realize that there are certain things that trigger sexual thoughts for me. Highly sexual scenes in movies, articles about sex in magazines... and I have learned that I need to be really careful about how much of that stuff I expose myself to, because it fuels what I think about for the next few hours or days, and it often stirs up feelings, emotions and desires that I then have to work through.

Keep grounded in the Bible

This sounds obvious, but seriously, the word of God is really powerful. Living in the culture that we do, we need to consistently remind ourselves of what God's plan is for healthy sexuality, because otherwise we will begin to believe what popular culture says about it.

Talk to your girlfriends

I have some amazing single friends in my life and we have decided to talk honestly about sex and the *not having* part. We share how we are going and what we are struggling with and we pray for each other and talk about what we've learned. It's so much easier to walk this road when you realize you're not walking alone.

Exercise

A lot of people find that regular exercise is quite helpful in just getting rid of excess 'energy'. Apparently there is a whole lot of scientific research out there that backs that up – something to do with endorphins being released. Whatever it is called, I think they may actually be onto something.

'Daughters of Jerusalem,
I charge you by the gazelles
and by the does of the field:
Do not arouse or awaken love
until it so desires.'

Song of Songs 3:5

Something to think about...

Do you remember the part in Song of Songs where the lead singer urges the women of Jerusalem to 'not awaken love until the time is right'? (Song of Songs 3:5) I've often wondered if many of us have *awakened* emotions and desires and thoughts prematurely because of the movies, TV and magazines that we've consumed? I could be interpreting it completely wrongly, but it's an interesting thought, because we do live in a highly sexualized culture and most of us started watching shows that had a great deal of sexual references in them and reading magazines which were pretty much *about* sex when we were in our early teens.

Shows like 'Sex and the City' (which we've all watched... for the clothes of course) completely distort what the Bible tells us is God's ideal for sex, and creates an illusion that sex is a selfish, no-strings-attached act which we are all entitled to do whenever we feel the urge. We've got to honestly consider how much of an effect these sorts of shows have had on us and our own sexuality and expectations.

I'm not saying that we should never watch TV or read magazines, but I do think it's something we need to consider. Is it possible to watch people having sex, talking about sex, telling lies about the meaning of sex and not have our own views on sex challenged or compromised? That's a question we each have to answer for ourselves. One thing I can tell you though is that it's highly likely that the more sex you watch and read about, the more you will feel ripped off, or that you're missing out.

How *to:*

Handle insensitive remarks

People say some really dumb things sometimes. Most of the time they don't mean any harm. In fact, most of the time when people bring up your singleness, their *intention* is to encourage you. It's just that most people don't really know what to say, so they end up using clichés and repeating meaningless statements that people told them when they were single.

These comments used to really annoy me, but I've since realized that they are inevitable and so now I try to approach them with a mixture of humor and grace. I've realized that they only bother me at those times I am feeling sensitive about being single. When I am in a position of enjoying the season I am in, I can shake them off easily. Here are some of my favourites...

'So you're still single?'

I've found this is one of the most frequent questions thrown around. It's the *still* that's the killer, I reckon. It implies that singleness is an undesirable affliction or disease, like 'Do you STILL have that cough?' or 'Are you STILL wearing that old sweater?'

Q: 'So you're still single?'

A: 'Yes, but don't worry it's not contagious.'

'Oh, so when's your turn?'

You generally encounter this one at weddings or engagement parties. The probability of being asked it increases exponentially if you are a bridesmaid or related to the bride or groom. If you're close by a dance floor you could always respond like this:

Q: 'Oh, so when's your turn?'

A: 'Around the dance floor? Now, actually.'

'Why are you single?' or
'I just don't know why you're single?'

This is a tough one to answer – because the only truthful way to answer it is probably going to expose a great deal of your heart and the sort of person who asks it is probably not the sort of person that you want to share your heart with. I'd suggest the best way to deal with this sort of comment is humor:

Q: 'Why are you single?'

A: 'I think it's my toenail collection – it really turns the guys off.'

'So, where's your man?'

Again, this is an unanswerable question, because if you knew where he was, you'd probably be there too!

Q: 'So, where's your man?'

A: 'I don't know, but if I see him around I'll be sure to let you know.'

'You're still so young' or 'You've got plenty of time.'

These sorts of comments are annoying because although they may be true, they don't take into account where you are at and what you are feeling. Pain and loneliness don't have an age. But it's difficult to tell someone that without sounding desperate and needy.

Q: 'You've got plenty of time.'

A: 'Yes, they say 40 is the new 20.'

'It will happen when you least expect it.'

This is probably my all time most hated *single* comment. Because (this is the way I think anyway) if I am going to get married, every day I live I am a day closer to meeting the guy I'm going to marry, so as time goes by how can I expect it less? I don't know who came up with that one, it's not even logical.

'Fools show their annoyance at once,

but the prudent overlook an insult.'

Proverbs 12:16

Myth No. 6:

Getting married is something that grown ups do. Isn't that what we thought when we were kids? I remember thinking that when you got married you became a *proper* adult, it was kind of like the seal of approval that said, 'Yes, you've finally reached adulthood. Welcome to the club.' The only problem is… what if you don't get married, or don't get married until you are a lot older. Does that make you less of an adult than your married peers?

If we perceive marriage as a rite of passage to adulthood we will struggle with our identity as adults until we are married. This can result in us approaching many things with an, 'Oh I couldn't do that,' attitude because in our minds we had planned to do them when we grew up and since we're not married, we're not proper grown ups yet. It can also result in a resistance to making long term plans and an inability to commit to anything for longer than six months because of the *what ifs*, and *just in case* I meet someone.

Ok, so here's my confession: I have suffered from an aversion to buying white goods. I guess in my mind it was one of those things that I imagined I would do when I got married. So although I have been living out of home for years, I had until recently, never actually owned any white goods. I'd managed to borrow a fridge from a friend but had no washing machine and so I (embarrassingly) returned to my parent's house each week to do my washing. Buying a washing machine just seemed like such a permanent, adult sort of thing to do, and in my mind it was one of those things you did when you got married. You'll be pleased to know that I just recently bought my first washing machine, (eBay is the way to go, people), and now I am relishing the fact that I can have clean clothes whenever I want.

> '...we all have our own, 'I'll do that when I'm married' scenario'

This whole episode got me thinking about how we all have our own, 'I'll do that when I'm married...' scenario. Yours may be different from mine. It could be to do with moving out of home, buying a house, going on a long term mission trip, committing to a church… It doesn't really matter what it is, it's just whatever you associate with being 'adult'.

The truth is though, as single women we are no less adult than the same-aged people around us who are married. Sure, they may have walked a part of their journey with a husband, but that doesn't automatically make them further ahead or *more* adult.

Adulthood is about taking full responsibility for our lives, for the decisions we make and for the way we choose to live. The only reason it is linked to marriage is because marriage often forces people to take on that responsibility. The fact is, we all have the opportunity to take ownership of our lives whether we are married or single. If we wait until we are married to grow up, we may find we remain teenagers for a disproportionately long time.

We're not second-class citizens just because we're not married. We all need to stop living with the mantra, 'When I'm married I'll... buy myself pretty underwear... go on that mission trip... start learning to cook...' Our lives are now. They are not a *practice run* for when we are married. They are *real and valid*. Embrace the fullness of what life has to offer *today*.

Formula
for meeting a
Man

There is no formula*.
Full Stop.
None.
End of Chapter.

*Just because your Mum and Dad met at a party and got engaged six weeks later (true story), or your best friend met her husband whilst on a mission trip to the Middle East (not a true story)... doesn't mean that this will happen for you. Don't let anyone deceive you - there is no formula. Some people say the guy has to pull the move. Others share stories of the girl proposing. All I know is that your best chance is to keep walking each day with Jesus and keep submitting each moment to Him and He'll lead you and guide you in the way that is best in your story.

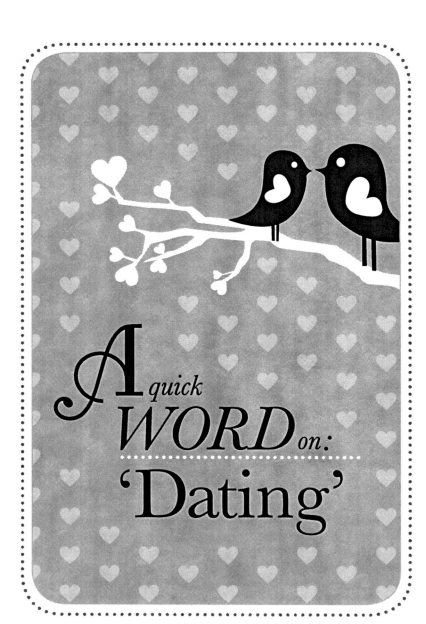

A _quick_
WORD _on:_
'Dating'

Warning: I'm about to make one of those big, generalized statements, so apologies if this doesn't include you, but I think it's a topic that we need to review. So here goes:

'Dating' is the new 'Engaged'

At least, that's what appears to be happening in many church circles. There seems to be a general consensus that before we 'go out' with someone we need to have done at least three months of pre-date groundwork, know how many kids they want and whether or not their personality type sits within the complementing quadrant of our own on the personality chart. Now, I'm not advocating for us to all rush out and give our hearts away to just anyone. However, I do wonder if it would be beneficial for us to have a slightly more flexible view on dating.

They tell me that back in the *good old days*, (read: when my parents were my age) it was quite normal to take a 'friend' to a party or a wedding without raising any eyebrows. It was something that everyone did and it was an acceptable way of meeting people and essentially *checking them out* in a public setting without any expectation of ongoing commitment. These days, if you rock up to a party with someone new, there is often an automatic assumption that you are *together* and in a serious committed relationship that will most likely end in marriage. The problem with this is that it discourages many of us from dating because we don't want people to assume we're seriously interested in someone when we don't even know that ourselves.

It's a bit of a dilemma really, because with the best intentions of creating an honorable culture of dating we have actually created a culture that in many ways prevents us from getting to know potential partners without it seeming like a 'big deal'. To be quite clear, I don't believe that dating, *just for the fun of it* is what we should be doing, but at the same time, we don't need to *know* that we are going to marry someone in order to go on a date (or two or three) with them.

The notion that we are all waiting for The One contributes to this behavior, because unless we know that someone is The One, we are reluctant to go on a date with them or even attempt to get to know them more. This type of thinking is problematic because, as many married couples will testify, we won't always *know* someone is The One until we truly get to know them and develop a deeper relationship with them. Perhaps, many of us are waiting for the 'lightning bolt' moment where God highlights The One with a spotlight from heaven, instead of recognizing that He just as often reveals His will over a period of time through a series of small confirmations.

All this is to say – you may not *know* at the very moment you meet someone that they are the person with whom you will spend the rest of your life. (Yes I know this does happen. My sister was one of *them*, but let's just admit that these kinds of encounters are generally the exception rather than the rule.) Therefore, it is hugely important not to write guys off straight away just because we 'don't think they're The One'. It is also worth spending time getting to know guys. Without exposing the deepest parts of our hearts, we can still go on dates and to parties, hang out and build friendships with guys in order to see whether they develop into something more.

One *more* thing...

I have had SO many long, and sometimes heated, conversations about whether it's 'ok' for girls to ask boys out. It comes up at dinner parties. I've talked about it late into the night with friends. I've had conversations with girls who are terrified that they will be doing the *wrong thing* if they ask a guy out but who are equally terrified of missing their opportunity if they don't. I've talked to guys who are baffled that girls are afraid of asking them out and other guys who vehemently argue that it is the man's role. Over the years I've pitched my tent in both camps.

> *I've talked to guys who are baffled that girls are afraid of asking them out and other guys who vehemently argue that it is the man's role*

All I can say is that I don't think there is a *right* or a *wrong* way. There is probably a more common way that things happen, (guys asking girls out), but just because something is more likely to happen doesn't mean that it is the correct or only way that things can be done. There is lots of teaching out there about dating and about not dating and about courtship and about men and women and how it's all meant to work. There are formulas and strategies and stories and rules and 3-step plans. Some of it is helpful and some of it not so much.

It's always worth remembering when we encounter this stuff that the Bible wasn't written as a 'How To' guide. The stories of marriage and romance in the Bible are not in there so that we can imitate and copy them. They are included primarily as part of a bigger story of God's interaction with humanity. What these stories reveal to us is that God cares about and moves through marriages.

When I studied biblical interpretation, our lecturer kept saying over and over that 'God moves in different ways in different days.' Meaning that just because God did things one way in the Bible, it doesn't mean that it is the only way He works. Let's not forget that our God is the God who is forever new and He is never bound by the ways that He has worked in the past.

...the Bible wasn't written as a 'How To' guide

That said, His character remains unchanged, so we can rest in the knowledge that He is still good, He still cares, and He still works powerfully through relationships.

God may have led Ruth to lie at the feet of Boaz, effectively proposing to him (one of the biggest pull-the-moves ever staged) but that doesn't mean that is God's plan for you. It may be... who knows? God asks people to do really weird things sometimes. On the other hand, just because Rebekah played a passive role within her story (while Ruth was pulling the big moves, Rebekah was just going about her everyday camel watering duty when she was *discovered* and chosen to be Isaac's wife) that doesn't mean that you're never allowed to show interest in a guy or ask to get to know him more. Always remember that for every Ruth there is a Rebekah.

BE RELEASED. You have the Holy Spirit living in you. Go with what you think God is telling you to do. Obviously be accountable. Talk things over with people who you respect and don't do anything that the Bible clearly says not to do! But seriously – stop being confined by cultural *rules* that may not have any biblical grounding anyway.

I find God's surprising-ness profoundly exciting! The fact that He is endlessly creative means that we don't have to expect our life story to happen the way someone else's has.

The
bit *at the*
END

I promised at the start that I wouldn't take too much of your time and I think that unless I stop writing soon, this book is in danger of becoming another one of the *unfinishables*. So I'll share with you two more thoughts and we'll be done.

The second last thing I want to say is that we are all different. Obvious – yes. But no less true. The fact that we're all different and we all see the world in a unique way is one of the things that I simultaneously love and hate. There is nothing better than having an 'Ahah!' moment with someone where you totally *get* each other. But at the same time, diversity of opinion and view can lead to such richness and depth of understanding.

...diversity of opinion and view can lead to such richness and depth of understanding.

The lenses through which I view life and God have been formed through the experiences that I have had. I have grown up in a particular home, in a particular community, gone to a particular school, worked at a particular job, attended a particular church, hung out with a particular set of friends... and all of these things have influenced the way that I see and interpret the world.

Your experiences will most likely have been different from mine which means that there were probably parts in this book to which you felt resistance. (Resistance could range from anywhere between thinking *that's not my experience,* to slamming the book shut in anger and yelling, *'That's SO not true! She has no idea.')*

My request is that you spend some time, even just a little bit, maybe when you're cleaning your teeth or something, thinking about *why* you disagree. Is it because of your cultural background? Your upbringing? Your church? Your past experiences? Or, is it because agreeing would require you to change?

The point of this is not so that you end up agreeing with me or seeing things from my point of view. It's so that you know, for yourself, why you believe what you believe. And why you are living the way you are living. When we take the time to think about why we are living the way we are, we are choosing to live intentionally (bike riding), rather than just waiting for circumstance and past experiences to direct us (bus stop).

Now, to my final thought - what's the one thing I want to leave you with? Well. A lot of thoughts are shooting across my mind: I could remind you that we're not victims to singleness; that life now is real and significant; I could stress the importance of facing and wrestling with the things that challenge us, always being aware that the grass is green not because of what side of the fence we are on but because of whether we water it or not.

But the one thought that stands out more than any other is this: I want you to know that *it is possible.*

Contentment. Joy. Full life. Wholeness... as a single woman.

Being able to honestly say that you are content and to mean it from the bottom of your heart. It is possible. Truly. I promise. It's not a mirage or a Christian cliché. But you need to know that most of the time you have to work at it. And you definitely need to choose it. You have to make conscious decisions to allow God to be God and to do His thing in His way and in His time.

But it *is* possible. So don't give up. And don't give in to the lies. No more standing around at the bus stop, waiting for life to begin. Because now is the time to jump on your bike and peddle your little heart out towards Jesus and His destiny in your life.

Happy *Riding!*

A word of thanks...

Thank you Jesus! You will always be my favorite. Thank you Cathie, your 'Do it, Taz' over hot jam donuts on a cold morning at the market was what got this whole thing started in the first place. Mum and Dad, thank you for *always* believing in me. And thank you Mum for all of the hours of editing, proof-reading, reading and re-reading that you did. I think you may have read this manuscript more times than I have! Thank you Brenton. A little bit of encouragement from you goes a long way. A million times thank you to the people who helped finance this project, you know who you are. Thank you to all of my friends (you also know who you are) who have listened to my rants over the years. Thank you for encouraging me in my journey and for believing that I could pull this off.

CPSIA information can be obtained at www.ICGtesting.com
Printed in the USA
BVOW02s1312221013

334371BV00007B/36/P